HOW TO BE BLESSED
& HIGHLY FAVORED

MICHELLE
McKINNEY HAMMOND

THORNDIKE PRESS

An imprint of Thomson Gale, a part of The Thomson Corporation

Detroit • New York • San Francisco • New Haven, Conn. • Waterville, Maine • London • Munich

THOMSON
✳ ™
GALE

LIBRARY OF CONGRESS CATALOGING-IN-PUBLICATION DATA

McKinney Hammond, Michelle, 1957–
    How to be blessed and highly favored / by Michelle McKinney Hammond.
      p. cm.
    Originally published: 1st ed. Colorado Springs, Colo. : WaterBrook Press, 2001.
      ISBN 0-7862-8872-8 (hardcover : alk. paper) 1. Christian life. 2. Large type books. I. Title.
    BV4501.3.M37 2006
    248.4—dc22
                                       2006014991

Published in 2006 by arrangement with WaterBrook Press, a division of Random House, Inc.

Printed in the United States of America on permanent paper
10 9 8 7 6 5 4 3 2 1

My heart, my soul, my everything
belongs to the One who has given His
all for me.
Lord, my most urgent prayer is that I
will be responsible
for more smiles on Your face than tears
from Your heart.
May I bless You in all I say and do.

To my parents and siblings
who are my greatest blessing and delight.
You bless my life with the most
important ingredient:
endless love.

CONTENTS

ACKNOWLEDGMENTS

To my new family at WaterBrook: I'm excited about our future together. Thank you for acknowledging my heart and insisting on passion.

Erin Healy: You, my precious editor, are an angel! Thank you for the questions, observations, and encouragement. Truly two are better than one. I thank God for you.

Laura Wright, my production editor, thank you for making me tell "it" like it is.

Chip McGregor, thank you for your constant sensitivity and care. And for arranging a beautiful marriage.

To the faithful twelve: You know who you are. Thank you for praying, pushing, prodding, provoking, listening, correcting . . . well . . . You know all that you do. You are loved and appreciated.

1. IT'S A WONDERFUL LIFE

EMBRACING THE CONCEPT OF EXTRA-DIMENSIONAL BLESSINGS

"Fear not, little flock; for it is your Father's good *pleasure* to *give* you the *kingdom.*"

Luke 12:32 (KJV)

The young man peered over the containers he was stacking to answer my question. "Sure, we carry that yogurt. As a matter of fact, I'm switching the merchandise on that brand right now. Here, take these. They're still good. Just tell them at the checkout that I said you could have them for free."

"Wow! Thanks," I said. Gleefully I headed toward the front of the store, my arms loaded with several pint-size containers. As I conveyed the message to the sales clerk, my girlfriend (who was ahead of me in line *paying* for her yogurt) said, "How do you always manage to do that? Girl, you must have an invisible sign on you somewhere that says, 'Give me everything for free!' "

I have a confession to make. I am spoiled.

11

Terribly, terribly spoiled. It's true. I have been the recipient of such freebies as yogurt, free rent, a beautiful baby grand piano, and well, you name it! And that's just the tangible, in-your-hands end of the spectrum. I could go on and on about God's loving guidance, His special way of letting me know I have His undivided attention (at least it feels that way), or the favor He gives me with others. I choose to name all these things gifts from God. Some of my blessings have been material, and others have been incredible opportunities that some would view as serendipitous moments, but I see my Father's hand in the midst of it all.

Looking back over my life, I can honestly say that God has pretty much given me everything I've ever asked Him for, from the easy to the seemingly impossible. My list of unfulfilled requests is a short one comprised of things I still anticipate receiving in His perfect time. Why am I so confident? It certainly isn't because I'm more spiritual than the next person. I know many people who pray more, read their Bible more, and simply know more about God than I do. On the contrary: As I have sought to understand why some folks are blessed more abundantly than others, God's Word has confirmed for me that His ultimate desire is for *all* of us to live a blessed life — one that overflows with His rich provision and goodness as we cooperate with His Spirit to become more and more like Christ. I also discovered that being a super-Christian is not a prerequisite to being super-blessed. There — now you can breathe a sigh of relief along with me! However, God's Word does give us some keys to accessing the deep riches of God's blessing, and I plan to share with you in the coming pages what I've learned.

"Blessed and highly favored!" That's the enthusiastic response I often receive when I ask people, "How are you?" It has become one of the favorite sayings of the day, a mantra of sorts as we seek to have a positive confession. This particular response, however, always gives me cause to pause and reflect. *Do these people really know what they're saying? Do they know what is required of them in order for that to be true? Do they understand that salvation is free, but blessings and favor on the level they speak of cost something?* You see, there are grace blessings, which are the basic provisions any good parent would give to his or her child, things like food, clothing, and shelter — the basics, with no extra trimmings. But then there are *bonus* blessings. *Extra-dimensional* blessings. Blessings above and beyond the normal ration we all can claim as believers. God makes these blessings available to us.

At a price.

I don't know anyone who doesn't want to be blessed abundantly. Yet it seems to me that some of us just wait around with the attitude that God owes us something. Why is this? He already paid a debt He did not owe in order to purchase our salvation. Still, many of His children have a "Santa Claus" mentality: If we are good enough . . . if we wait long enough . . . plead loud enough . . . believe hard enough . . . blessings will miraculously rain down upon us from heaven.

I submit to you that we've missed the truth about what is really required of us in order to get those extra goodies. Are there really secrets to tapping into the reserve of God? Indeed there are! Does God really want to bless you? You'd better believe it! But God wants something from you, too. You say you want the favor of God on your life? Well you've got some homework to do. In order to access His extra-dimensional blessings, you need to equip yourself with knowledge. You've got to find out who has the blessings you're looking for (that should be God), how to find Him, and what He

14

requires from you in order to do something about your request. What are blessings? What is favor? And who has the key to the storehouse of these things? What motivates God to give us access to the things we desire? All these questions and more must be answered before we can enter into the abundant life that God wants for every believer.

SEEING IS BELIEVING

Speaking of believing, what do you believe? Your answer is important if you want to be blessed and highly favored.

And without faith it is impossible to please God, because anyone who comes *to him* must believe that he exists and that he rewards those who earnestly *seek him.* (Hebrews 11:6)

Another translation says those who *diligently* seek Him. I'll assume — because you're reading this book — that you believe God exists, but do you believe God is really who He says He is? That He can really do what He says He can do? Do you believe that He really rewards those who seek Him? The "name it, claim it, and frame it" and the "confess it and possess it" schools of theology have caused many to focus their faith on the desired *object* or *result* in order to make their dreams come true. But I submit to you that the focus has been misplaced. Our gaze must be upon *Him,* the one who holds the key to the manifestation of all our dreams and desires. Do you believe that He is willing and able to fulfill His promises to you? To uphold every blessing He has promised in His Word? Only if you believe He is telling the truth will He be pleased with you. If you want a gift from the Giver, you must first be pleasing to Him. You must be someone He wants to give a gift to.

To be unsure whether God will keep His Word is to call Him a liar. Think about it. How does it make you feel when people behave as if they don't trust you to keep your promise to them? Their attitude doesn't exactly put you in the mood to do what you've said you'd do, does it? You think, *Well, forget it then. Why should I bother?* But you are happy to do anything for those who trust you completely. After all, these people are counting on you! You've got a standard to live up to. Their confidence might actually inspire you to push the envelope, to go the extra mile. You get a kick out of surprising them. It gives you pleasure to surpass their expectations. And so it is with God.

OH, CURSES!

In order for us to appreciate the full implication of a blessing, a comparison with curses is in order. God tells us in Deuteronomy 30:19 to *choose* blessings or curses. Now why would He tell us to choose if we didn't have a choice? And what exactly is a curse anyway? Besides the usual implication of profanity, my friend Webster says that a curse is misfortune that occurs when someone calls upon evil to bring harm or retribution to another. But I say that scriptural evidence points to *God's disregard* as the "curse" that allows us to fail when we rely on our own devices. What would cause us to be disregarded by God? Allowed by Him to fail? To struggle in the midst of unanswered prayer? The psalmist makes it clear:

If I regard wickedness [iniquity] in my
heart,
The Lord will not hear;
But certainly God has heard;
He has given heed to the voice of my
prayer.
Blessed be God,
Who has not turned away my prayer,

Nor His lovingkindness from me.
(Psalm 66:18–20, NASB)

Two scriptures lead me to believe that iniquity is at least two steps beyond your garden-variety sin:

And the LORD passed by before him, and proclaimed, "The LORD, The LORD God, merciful and gracious, longsuffering, and abundant in goodness and truth, keeping mercy for thousands, forgiving iniquity and transgression and sin." (Exodus 34:6–7, KJV)

Seventy weeks are determined upon thy people and upon thy holy city, to finish the *transgression,* and to make an end of sins, and to make reconciliation for *iniquity.* (Daniel 9:24, KJV)

Sin is when you aim for the mark (righteousness) and miss it; transgression is when you acknowledge the mark but choose to do your own thing anyway. At both of these stages repentance is still readily in reach. But when iniquity sets in, repentance is harder to choose. Why? Because when you remove the standard, any sense of conviction goes out the window. After all, why should you repent for something that you don't believe is wrong? Based on my study, iniquity occurs when you decide the mark is not real or doesn't apply to you. You set your own standards. You declare, "Well, this is just the way I am — take it or leave it." Well, God chooses to leave it if your behavior doesn't line up with His Word. He will not partner with those who willfully disobey Him. He is far too holy for that. So He invites us to choose, to intentionally aim for His mark of righteousness. Do you want Him to be a participant and helper in your life, or do you want to strike out on your own? The choice is yours.

If you consider yourself a victim of generational curses, this concept might be hard for you to grasp. But again I say, why would God ask you to choose if you couldn't? The believer must understand that Jesus annihilated generational curses on the tree at Calvary. He became cursed in order to set us free from any curse that sought to claim us. What is now in effect are the consequences of patterns of generational *behavior.* Many of us adopt the less-than-victorious habits of our parents or grandparents because it seems like the "normal" thing to do, even though we reap the same disastrous results they did. That is not the hand of God smiting with a curse; that is simply the consequence of our unwise actions. On the other hand, through Christ we are free to have our lives transformed by the renewing of our minds (Romans 12:2). As our habits change, so does our harvest.

Even back in the Old Testament, God was quick to say that a curse would not alight on those who don't deserve it (Proverbs 26:2). He used Jeremiah and Ezekiel to tell the people to stop repeating the proverb that the children's teeth were on edge because their parents had eaten sour grapes (Jeremiah 31:29–30; Ezekiel 18:2–4). Each person, parent, or child, would be responsible for paying the penalty of his or her own sins. So there! You see, even back then, the scripture about God visiting the iniquity of the parents up to the fourth generation had been greatly misunderstood. His intention was not to bind people, but to halt the disintegration of society by not allowing self-destructive cycles to continue beyond the fourth generation. This explains the Israelites' cycle of repentance and disobedience throughout the Old Testament. Because of our right to choose, God had to set boundaries so we wouldn't permanently damage ourselves! This generational limitation became His way of stopping the madness, and He made the promise that He would love those who loved Him and hate those who hated him. So when the iniquities of your forefathers come to "visit" you, treat them like any other unwanted guest: Don't let them in!

Sometimes we are victims of others' sins because we find ourselves in the wrong place at the wrong time. In these cases we might say we are victims of circumstance but not curses. It is important to understand that we do indeed inherit genetic traits from our parents that predispose us to areas of weakness and strength (health and temperament-wise), but such predisposition is not God-imposed. Through God's power at work within us, we can claim victory over generational patterns, including health matters, as we remain attentive and obedient to the Holy Spirit's guidance in our everyday lives. A famous preacher tells of how he severed the chain binding him to his family's history of diabetes by changing the way he ate. Overcoming curses is not always that simple, but sometimes, after considering the ways of our parents and our parents' parents, we can effectively put our lives on a different path. It is just too easy to simply place the blame elsewhere instead of taking responsibility for our own lives. Remember this story?

And His disciples asked Him, saying, "Rabbi, who sinned, this man or his parents, that he should be born blind?"

Jesus answered, "It was neither that this man sinned, nor his parents; but it was in order that the works of God might be displayed in him." (John 9:2–3, NASB)

This man's misfortune was not anyone's fault. Through Jesus' eyes the situation looked completely different. Just as He described the death of Lazarus as mere sleep, Jesus saw the opportunity here to reverse an unfortunate natural circumstance and display God's power through the miracle of divine healing! God wants to demonstrate His power in our lives as well. So it is important to remember that misfortune and failure are not God's preference; therefore, He would never willingly cause the innocent to suffer for what someone else did. So much for curses.

THANK GOD FOR BLESSINGS!
What exactly is a blessing anyway? Well, Webster says that a blessing is the act of one who blesses. It is approval, encourage-

ment, a thing conducive to happiness or welfare, or grace said at a meal. But to bless someone is to hold him or her in reverence, to hallow or consecrate by religious rite or word, to invoke divine care for or confer prosperity or happiness upon a person, or to protect and preserve him. While curses enable us to fail, blessings enable us to have success. That sounds good to me! I'll choose blessings over curses any day of the week!

We've been told to revere God, but did you ever stop to consider that God reveres *us?* He considers us an awesome creation of His hand. The angels are certainly still speechless as they consider the work of redemption that God was moved to do on our behalf. Sacrificing His own Son? How could we possibly be worth all of that, especially the way some of us behave? Yet God is fiercely passionate about us coming into the fullness of the inheritance He has set aside for us. He is not willing that any should perish. For this reason God is willing to allow the fullness of time to pass in order to redeem as many as possible. Let's face it, there must be times when He feels like pulling the plug on us when He witnesses some of the things that go on down here. But He doesn't.

Now that is grace to the utmost.

God gives us the promise of His divine care for us in spite of ourselves. He chooses to extend His riches and His joy to us in order to glorify Himself. Why? Not to gain our approval, but simply because He loves us. He wants to protect and preserve us until the day we meet in eternity and finally become one with Him. However, God is a practical God. He understands what it takes to live a good life in the natural sense, and He wants us to be fully equipped to live victoriously and abundantly. He does not treat us like unwanted stepchildren. He is a generous and benevolent Father who gains pleasure from blessing His children. Small wonder that David sought his Father's heart:

I lift up my eyes to you,
to you whose throne is in heaven.
As the eyes of slaves look to the hand of
their master,
as the eyes of a maid look to the hand
of her mistress,
so our eyes look to the LORD our God,
till he shows us his mercy.

(Psalm 123:1–2)

Well, what's God to do when it's put to Him

like that? How could He let David down?

David was counting on Him completely, almost helplessly. No one with compassion can ignore another who so humbly states his case. Someone who is totally dependent upon and trusting in you. The now-famous prayer of Jabez also came from a heart that was totally reliant on the sovereign hand of God.

> Jabez cried out to the God of Israel, "Oh, that you would bless me and enlarge my territory! Let your hand be with me, and keep me from harm so that I will be free from pain." And God granted his request. (1 Chronicles 4:10)

Again, Jabez's belief that only the hand of God could accomplish what he needed moved the heart of God to answer Jabez's prayer.

Innumerable occasions and prayers throughout Scripture could be cited to prove this resounding point — God wants to bless us. He wants to prosper us. He wants to grant us divine protection. God wants to show up in our world and make His presence known to others by the things that He makes manifest in our lives. This is His desire for us individually, as well as corporately, as a body of worshipers. Our ability to be blessed affects kingdom business. He knows the world is looking for evidence of Him among His people. He longs to make us the envy of all who don't know Him in order to provoke them to seek relationship with Him.

Take a minute to consider how He had Moses bless the people in a most significant way as they headed through enemy territory toward the Promised Land:

> The Lord said to Moses, "Tell Aaron and his sons, 'This is how you are to bless the Israelites. Say to them:
> " ' "The LORD bless you
>   and keep you;
> the LORD make his face shine upon you
>   and be gracious to you;
> the LORD turn his face toward you
>   and give you peace." '
> "So they will put my name on the
>   Israelites, and I will bless them."
>   (Numbers 6:22–27)

"The Lord bless you and keep you." But in order for Him to do that He must be looking at you. And when He looks at you He must be pleased. He must be inspired to be gracious to you. He has got to like what He sees. As long as He is looking at you, you can have the peace that surpasses all understanding. Because as long as He is looking at you, you can be sure that you are basking under the watchful eye of His protection. Oh, but when He looks away, the enemy of your soul can have a field day. He gets in his licks while God is not looking.

Now that doesn't mean that God doesn't see what's going on. It merely feels like it when He withdraws and declares, "I'm not touching that." He will only participate in what pleases Him — that is, when you're pressing toward the mark for the prize found in the high calling of Christ Jesus. But He becomes a sideline spectator when we dash down the field of life the wrong way, leaving plenty of room for Satan, our opponent, to tackle us.

So if blessings are all about having God's undivided attention, then surely favor is basking in the smile of God. Yes, when we make God smile, things happen! When we tickle the heart of God, He can't help Himself. He's got to show up and show out on your behalf! When God smiles, His favor flows toward us.

DO ME A FAVOR
What is *favor* exactly? As usual, my buddy

Webster is ready with an answer. He profoundly states that a favor is friendly regard shown to another by a superior, approving consideration or attention, partiality, gracious kindness, leniency, effort in one's behalf or interest, attention, a token of love (usually worn conspicuously), or to do a kindness for, to treat gently or carefully, to give support or confirmation to, to afford advantages for success to — well, well, well! I don't know about you, but I am only that way with my friends. People I know. People I have walked with and talked with for a while. I've established a sense of trust with these people. We have bonded big time!

Don't you want God's tokens of love to be conspicuous in your life? Don't you want Him to afford advantages to you for your success? I most certainly do! But I also understand and dare to say that favors and the extent of their greatness are based entirely on the quality of the relationship. I may be telling too much of my business here, but I'm not too inclined to do a favor for just anybody unless the Holy Spirit prompts me. In today's culture you never know what you might be getting yourself into. Let's face it, if you were walking down the street and a stranger rushed up to you and said, "Do me a favor, loan me a hundred dollars right quick," you would look at them as if they were absolutely out of their mind. "I don't know you!" would probably be among your first words. But if a friend called you and made the same request, you probably wouldn't hesitate to hand it over if you could. After all, you know where your friend lives. But above and beyond that, you trust that person. Depending on the depth of your friendship, you might even give it without looking for it to be returned.

Well, God's got whatever it is that you need in the area of a favor. And He is more than willing to give it to you if your relationship with Him is in the right place. Can He trust you? Have you been such a great friend that He would be moved to give to you abundantly? What type of friend is God looking for? What makes Him sit up and take notice of us? What makes Him say to us what He said to Moses?

So the LORD said, "I have pardoned them according to your word." (Numbers 14:20, NASB)

Wow! You mean that we can influence God? Most definitely, if we are counted among His friends. John Wesley writes of Exodus 33:11, "And the Lord spake to Moses face to face as a man speaketh to his friend — which intimates not only that God revealed himself to Moses with greater clearness than to any other of the prophets, but also with greater expressions of particular kindness than to any other. He spake not as a king to a subject, but as a *man to his friend,* whom he loves, and with whom he takes sweet counsel."

What a glorious place to be! Intimate, exchanging ideas with God, reveling in the security that God is your friend. You are reconciled to Him through Jesus Christ, and now you have access to His throne. He anticipates your desires. You are free to make them known. He actually listens and does something about what you say if He's in agreement. And if He is not, well, you are such great friends that you don't mind being corrected by Him because you know that whatever He says is in your best interest. After all, He *does* know what is best, and *true* friends mirror one another's hearts and trust one another completely.

So what was it about those folks like Abraham, Moses, Joseph, David, and Daniel (just to name a few) that caught God's eye? What made them so special that He was moved to bless them so generously with wealth, prominent positions, and incredible legacies? What was it about Rahab, Ruth, Hannah, Abigail, the Shunnamite woman, the woman with the issue of blood, Esther, and Mary?

Mary!

Okay. Can we talk about Mary for a minute? Have you ever just put your hand on your hip and asked, "Why Mary? Why was Mary chosen to be the mother of Jesus?" If you're religious you've probably never wondered. But since I am slightly inclined to be nosy — just slightly — these are the sort of questions I ask. Of course, I don't have enough room to talk about all the people in the Bible that God gave the blessed-and-highly-favored nod to, so for the sake of the points I want to make in this book, I would like us to focus on Mary. After all, she is the one dubbed "blessed and highly favored" by Gabriel the angel. And since angels only repeat what God says, that indeed makes it official.

What was it about Mary that made God say, "I like her. I am going to grant her the blessing and favor that every single woman in Israel wants. Yep, she's the one to bear the Redeemer of Israel." Think about it. One day I heard someone musing: "If two football teams are playing against each other, and both are Christians, and both have prayed for God to help them win, how does He decide which team should get the victory?" Good question. One team will win and one will lose. Does it mean God likes the winning team better? Of course not. All determinations are made in accordance with God's kingdom purposes. When we are friends with God, we walk in the understanding that kingdom purposes should always take precedence over personal desires. The question is, Have we completely surrendered our personal desires to God? Do we trust His friendship enough to accept His determination and position on matters that concern us? When God selects someone to be a prominent player in the scheme of kingdom business, His selection is always based upon specific criteria.

That brings us back to Mary. I believe her conversation with Gabriel and her subsequent actions give us a lot of hints as to why God chose her to be "blessed among women." We can all take a clue from Mary and find ourselves also blessed. The blood of Jesus qualifies all of us to be friends with God, to expect His favor and His blessing upon our lives.

If we are willing to pay the price.

A Tale of Two Children

Consider the following scenario. In the center of this real-life drama is a father who has two children. One feels that the father owes him everything simply because he is a member of the family. This child does not pay much attention to the father. He merely calls or shows up when he needs something. He pouts and insults the father when he doesn't receive what he requested. The father, being a good father, does his paternal duty by supplying the basic necessities this child needs: food, provision, a home, help in time of trouble . . . you know — the bare essentials. Yet, this child always feels denied. This child will never feel blessed. This child has issues, issues that will grow like cancer if he does not deal with them by repenting. This child must ultimately make a true effort toward reconciliation in order to move the heart of his father.

On the other hand, this other child truly loves the father. This child is quite different. This child spends time with the father . . . does things to make the father happy . . . brings the father gifts . . . constantly showers the father with praise and love. This child brings a smile to the father's face. For this child, the father always seeks extra ways to show him how much he appreciates and treasures their relationship. He gives this child extra gifts, takes note of the wishes uttered even in idle conversation. He wants this child to know that he is interested in everything concerning him.

Now don't get me wrong. The father loves both children, but one is selfish, the other selfless. There is something appealing about someone who has a giving spirit, someone who seeks to please and not to get. This kind of spirit is limitless in what it can do. It can also move hearts of stone. And if it can move hearts of stone, how much more can it move the heart of God, our heavenly Father?

Since we all come from a family, whether father or mother is present or absent, we can all relate to the situation I just described. Every family has one. Yeah, I'm talking about the favorite. But why is that person the favorite? In the midst of the seeming contest is always something that is clearly evident: One child curries the favor of the parent; another merely expects it. Expectations without actions are never enough.

Take Cain and Abel for instance. Abel gave God, his heavenly Father, a tithe or offering of the fatty cuts of meat from the first of his best lambs, so God looked on Abel and his offering with favor. Cain, on the other hand, gave God an offering he considered good enough, but it was not what God wanted. God had clearly established in the garden (after the fall of Adam and Eve) that a blood sacrifice was necessary for approaching him. So Abel honored God by bringing what He had asked for. But the produce Cain brought to God was not received because the ground was cursed. It was an unacceptable tithe, for it merely represented the fruit of his own efforts versus a heart that revered God's covenant. Cain became upset when God did not respond with favor to what he'd brought. When Cain's countenance displayed his resentment, God asked him a very profound question:

Why are you angry? Why is your face downcast? If you do what is right, will you not be accepted? (Genesis 4:6–7)

Cain's actions clearly communicated his response. Instead of adjusting his attitude and changing his approach to God, and instead of giving God what He was looking for, Cain chose to blame Abel for his troubles: Cain asked Abel to go out to the field with him, and there, Cain murdered him! When confronted by God about his actions, Cain refused to confess or repent. He felt his sin was justified, just as his father, Adam, did in the garden. As far as Cain was concerned, it was God's fault for choosing favorites; never mind his own disobedience. For Cain, the consequences were not pretty.

The LORD said, "What have you done? Listen! Your brother's blood cries out to me from the ground. Now you are under a curse and driven from the ground, which opened its mouth to receive your brother's blood from your hand. When you work the ground, it will no longer yield its crops for you. You will be a restless wanderer on the earth."

Cain said to the LORD, "My punishment is more than I can bear. Today you are driving me from the land, and I will be hidden from your presence; I will be a restless wanderer on the earth, and whoever finds me will kill me."

But the LORD said to him, "Not so; if anyone kills Cain, he will suffer vengeance seven times over." Then the LORD put a mark on Cain so that no one who found him would kill him. So Cain went out from the LORD's presence and lived in the land

There you have it. When we justify our stubbornness, we end up being shocked by the magnitude of the consequences — although we shouldn't be. Perhaps we hope against hope that we will somehow escape the repercussions of our actions. Or we think that if God is a God of compassion then surely He will let us slide this time. But this issue has nothing to do with His compassion and everything to do with our obedience. Whether it is obedience in tithing or obedience in another area, we cannot expect to be blessed if we are not willing to do what is required of us by God. You see, when God withdraws his regard, failure is enabled only to be followed shortly by our heart's true desires going unfulfilled.

Even Cain understood the weighty implications of being separated from God. But God, ever the responsible Father, assured Cain that he would still have His protection and basic blessings of necessity, but without any fancy perks. No extra rewards. Yet it all would have been so simple. If only Cain had turned to Abel and said, "Hey, where did you get that unblemished, fatted lamb? Where can I get one?" If only Cain had dealt with his shortcomings, repented, and given God what He wanted, the story could have had a drastically different ending. If only . . .

The story of Cain and Abel rings true in too many modern day lives. Many of us want the favor and extra-dimensional blessings of God, but we are unwilling to go the extra mile or pay the price required to gain them. Instead when we observe others being blessed, we become disgruntled and discount the steps they took to get the blessing. Or worse yet, we accuse God of being unfair — which means that we still haven't dealt with ourselves and the part we played or didn't play in our own disappointment. Many of us chafe at, or completely disregard, God's instructions for tithing, righteous living, and covenant relationships, then wonder why we are unable to reach the realm of higher blessing and favor. The truth of the matter is this: Based on our own disobedience, known or unknown, we are simply not in the right position to receive.

This point was brought home to me by a recent experience. A friend of mine and I were comparing the features on our Palm Pilots. I decided that I wanted one of the programs he had on his, so he prepared to download it by beaming it to my Palm. We had our units face each another, and he hit the appropriate button. His unit flashed the message "searching . . . searching . . . searching . . ." My unit flashed the message, "waiting for sender . . . waiting for sender . . . waiting for sender . . ." After a while he grew impatient and moved. My unit flashed the message: "Connection has been broken." To help figure out why the transfer didn't work, I tried to beam his Palm. As soon as I hit the appropriate button, the message flashed "Searching . . ." His unit displayed "Waiting for sender . . ." Meanwhile another friend present asked if I had everything turned on correctly. I insisted, "Of course!" But at that same moment my unit flashed, "Your option to beam has been turned off. Would you like to turn it on?" Well! After recovering from my surprise, I pressed "yes," and the transfer of data to his Palm was successfully accomplished. However, I was never able to receive a program from him. When I got home I examined my user manual to learn how to solve our beaming problem and discovered that we were holding our units in the wrong position.

What's the point? God is searching . . . searching . . . searching for someone to give a blessing to. He really does want to bless us and give us incredible gifts! Meanwhile we are waiting . . . waiting . . . waiting . . .

for a blessing. Sometimes while God is preparing to download a blessing to us, our impatience causes us to move, and the connection is broken. Other times we are not in the right position to receive what He has for us. He said, "My people are destroyed for lack of knowledge" (Hosea 4:6). Some of us think we're open to receive from God, but our option to receive may have been turned off by our disobedience. That disobedience separates us from Him and damages the line of communication needed to secure the blessing. Of course, we don't always deliberately cause a disconnection. Many of us have just not checked the manual — God's Word — to obtain the knowledge about how this blessing thing works and about how to get in the right position.

Somebody reading this is now thinking, *Well where does God's grace come into all of this?* I'll tell you where:

For *by grace* are ye saved through faith; and that not of yourselves: it is the gift of God: Not of works, lest any man should boast. (Ephesians 2:8, KJV)

You have already been given an extraordinary free gift that you did not deserve. Getting hold of the extras is up to you. Don't confuse sovereign acts of God with free blessings. There is a big difference. Remember extra-dimensional blessings minus our human devices are called miracles.

TIME TO CHOOSE

Have you simply been expecting God to bless you and now are wondering why nothing has been happening? Or maybe you've experienced a little taste of the blessed life and you long for more. Well, today is your day. We are about to cross the great divide, to switch from black and white to living color, from mediocre to incredible, from merely existing to really living, living in the fullness of what God desires for all of His children because He loves us so.

We are going to take it up a notch, stage a revolution in the spirit, and step into the extra-dimensionally blessed life. The highly favored life. Ah yes, it's a wonderful life! It can be your life when you link your faith to actions. Remember: Faith without works is dead, dead, dead! Don't just sit around waiting for God to bless you and complain under your breath when everything remains the same. Stop simply expecting and start pulling on heaven's windows and doors. Start tapping into the

41

heart of God and currying favor from His hand.

Did you know being blessed is up to you? Mm-hm, it's true. God has left it up to you to determine whether you will be in a position to be blessed.

> This day I call heaven and earth as witnesses against you that I have set before you *life* and death, blessings and curses. Now *choose life.* (Deuteronomy 30:19)

Choose blessings! God is in the blessing business, but you've got to be standing in the right spot. I don't know anyone who would deliberately choose curses and death, yet many do so out of ignorance. It is time to be illuminated so you can make the right choices. To learn valuable lessons from those who attained the blessed and favored life in order to imitate them and gain the same, or even greater, results. I think I've chatted this up enough. Let's get down to the meat of the matter — how to be blessed and highly favored. As I mentioned earlier, to coin the title of a popular movie, there's something about Mary, and we're about to find out exactly what it is.

THOUGHTS TO PONDER

- Is God your friend or just an acquaintance?

- Do you really know Him? Does He know you?

- How would you describe your friendship with God?

- Do you think God owes you? Do you curry his favor or are you merely expecting it?

- Are you doing things that make God want to turn His face away from you, or do you make Him smile?

- What can you do to improve your relationship with God?

2. THE ISSUE OF PURITY

LIVING FOR THE ONE YOU BELONG TO

In the sixth month, God sent the angel Gabriel to Nazareth, a town in Galilee, to a virgin pledged to be married to a man named Joseph, a descendant of David. The virgin's name was Mary.

Luke 1:26–27

Don't you find it interesting that the first thing the Bible tells us about Mary is where she lived and that she was a virgin? Oh, I can hear the collective groan already: Gee, we were having a good time. Why'd you have to go and spoil the mood by bringing up virginity and purity?

When I was a kid I decided I would eat my vegetables first and get them out of the way so I could enjoy the rest of my meal. I hated vegetables! As long as I could see them sitting there next to my sweet potatoes, they just took the joy out of my eating experience. I think sometimes we view les-

44

sons on holiness and purity just as we do those vegetables. The topic makes us nervous. It just takes all the joy out of the service because suddenly we are forced to face something that we do not like — the fact that not one of us is perfect. "As it is written: 'There is no one righteous, not even one' " (Romans 3:10).

That's why God's mercies are new every morning. His grace is eternally permanent, but when we open our eyes every morning, He pours out fresh mercy because He already knows that somewhere along the way we're going to need it. We are going to mess up in thought, word, or deed before the day is over, and His mercy is ready and waiting to meet the occasion. What a loving Father! God anticipates our failures and has a ready-made solution for our problems. His mercy is there to equip us to continue in His grace. It is there to help us have the strength to lay aside the things that so easily beset us and finally get the victory. He is rooting for us to make it.

Those fresh mercies are like a welcome glass of cool water. When we falter in the race or completely fall down, God is standing there, holding the water to our lips, inviting us to take a long swig. "Come on," He says, "don't give up now. You can do it.

My grace is sufficient for you. Take a drink of My mercy, refresh yourself and keep going." He is our greatest cheerleader. And our greatest helper. It is only by His spirit that we can be what He longs for us to be: whole and holy in His sight. Holiness is important to God. Why? Because we were made to reflect His image to the world, and God is, first and foremost, holy.

FIRST THINGS FIRST

I believe that when the Holy Ghost inspired men to write the Word of God, He didn't mince words. No, no. He dictated what was on His mind and made it plain what was of utmost importance to Him. Every word was deliberately placed, in precise order, for His point to ring loud and true. The first thing God says about Mary is that she lived in Nazareth and she was a virgin.

You know how people are when you ask about a young lady. They usually say, "Oh, she's a nice girl!" Well, God went beyond obvious externals to the intimate details. Mary was a virgin. She had kept herself pure. She had kept herself separate, awaiting a promise. She was pledged to be married to Joseph, a descendant of the house of David.

We, too, are pledged to be married. We

are the collective bride of Christ. He looks forward to His wedding day with great anticipation. Until then, His hope is that we will keep ourselves pure for Him, that we will keep ourselves separate from the things that court our flesh. He hopes we will conduct ourselves as a good fiancée should, doing nothing to stir up the jealousy of the One she loves. To stir up His jealousy is to offend Him. Offense will separate us from Him, inhibit our intimacy, and sour the courtship.

Trust me, no one feels like sending flowers and giving gifts when the courtship is shaky.

It's safe to say that one reason Mary kept herself separate was because she was aware she was promised to another. Are you walking in the awareness that you are promised to another? That you are promised to Christ? Most of us do not usually keep this thought at the front of our minds. It is hard to be mindful of One whom you cannot see. It is even harder to think of being promised to One with whom you've never had physical contact. Yet, whether married or single, we have been spoken for by a heavenly Lover — our match made by a heavenly Father. We are to walk as if we belong to Someone in honor of that promise.

One night I had a dream that I was in a place where I.D. cards were required. Everyone had one but me. After ransacking my purse and other belongings in an effort to find my own, I came up empty-handed. I felt out of place with no way to verify my identity, so I decided to play the whole thing off by pretending I had just misplaced my I.D.

"I don't know where my I.D. card is," I said. "My husband must have it."

"Your husband?" someone said. "You don't have a husband."

"Yes, I do," I countered defensively, embarrassed that someone was on to me and knew I was single.

"What is his name?" the person asked, narrowing her eyes. I paused. I was stuck, about to be completely uncovered, when a thought struck me. My eyes brightened, and a smile slowly spread across my face.

"J. C. Lord," I said with emphasis on each letter and word. (Jesus Christ Lord — get it?) Then, as the realization of what that meant really hit me, I straightened up in full confidence and announced once again, "Yes, that's right. J. C. Lord. I'm Mrs. Lord!" I could no longer contain my mirth. A giggle escaped my lips as I looked at the stupefied expression of my interrogator.

I awoke still chuckling. "Wow, Lord," I said. "So many times I forget that my identity is really hidden in You, that I am Your beloved and intended. Thank You for reminding me." I found myself reveling in that knowledge for the rest of the day. What a difference it made in my attitude to know that I was promised to and possessed by One so great.

FILL 'ER UP!

When you meet someone who is engaged, you may be struck by the fact that his or her entire existence is geared toward the wedding day — saving money for the wedding, dieting, working out, preparing that body for the honeymoon night. Everything is focused on being one's best for the big day and the days to follow. The flirtations and invitations of members of the opposite sex could just as well be water rolling off the back of a duck; engaged people have eyes and ears only for their intended. They are just not interested in anything or anyone who would distract them from getting to the church on time. Their lamps are full, so to speak.

But those who don't focus on the reality of one day seeing Christ and uniting with Him are like the foolish virgins in Matthew

25 who fell asleep on the job. Unprepared for the journey and weary of waiting for the groom, they awoke with a start to find themselves lacking the oil they needed to get to the wedding feast. The virgins who were serious about getting to the wedding had enough. They were prepared to go the distance. In the face of those who were not, their attitude was: "Hey, it's every woman for herself. Sorry. Can't help you. See ya, wouldn't wanna be ya!" When the groom finally arrived, the women who were not ready were left behind.

And so it is with us. It is up to us individually to arrive at the wedding. No one else will be able to help us get there. How seriously do you take your wedding day with Christ? Something is required of us now in order to see Him then, at the wedding feast. And that is merely the beginning of what is required in order to receive the blessings He wants to bestow on your life.

> Who may ascend the hill of the LORD?
>   Who may stand in his holy place?
> He who has *clean hands and a pure heart,*
>   who does not lift up his soul to an idol
>   or swear by what is false.
> *He will receive blessing from the LORD*

and vindication from God his Savior.
(Psalm 24:3–5)

Surely God is good to Israel,
   to those who are *pure* in heart.
(Psalm 73:1)

Blessed are the *pure* in heart,
   for they will see God.
(Matthew 5:8)

Who are the pure in heart? Those who do not delight in or serve the works of the flesh but instead walk after the mandates of the Spirit. Those who do not harbor unforgiveness, sexual immorality, impurity, anger, hatred, jealousy, envy, idolatry, selfishness, and the like. We've got to take out the trash, so to speak, and get rid of the things that God considers filthy. In order to be blessed we must purify our hearts and our hands. We must put ourselves in the position to see God. To be pleasing in His sight. The extra-dimensional blessings abide in His presence. We gain access to them when we remove everything from our lives that separates us from Him. We must roll up our sleeves and be willing to do the work of repentance.

Mary was pure in heart. Her actions

reflected this. She set herself apart. And God showed up in her personal world and blessed her. Many will say as they slide across the grace of God, "Well, God knows my heart." He sure does, and it doesn't take a lot of guesswork to figure out the attitudes and beliefs we harbor.

How can you who are evil say anything good? For out of the overflow of the *heart* the mouth speaks. The good man brings good things out of the good stored up in him, and the evil man brings evil things out of the evil stored up in him. (Matthew 12:34–35)

God is not moved by our good intentions; He is moved by our obedience to Him. As far as God is concerned, what you say and do reflects what is going on in your heart. And though He loves us enough to invite us to come as we are, He loves us too much to leave us in our former condition. He wants to be in fellowship with us, yet He cannot stand the stench of sin. Have you ever been trapped in a close space with someone who had bad body odor? It's enough to make you pass out. You can't wait to get out of that person's presence. That's how God feels about being near us in our sinfulness.

Therefore, He wants us to clean up our acts. That is why He hands us the Grace soap and a Mercy sponge and tells us to get busy!

Let us draw near to God with a sincere heart in full assurance of faith, having our *hearts* sprinkled to *cleanse* us from a guilty conscience and having our bodies washed with pure water. (Hebrews 10:22)

Come near to God and he will come near to you. Wash your hands, you sinners, and purify your *hearts,* you double-minded. (James 4:8)

Why is it so important that you embrace purity? Because it is the portal through which you must step to get to the blessed life! Small wonder the psalmist said, "If I had cherished sin in my heart, the Lord would not have listened" (Psalm 66:18). He knew he must first be what God wanted him to be before God would do what he wanted. To ask God to bless us when we do not honor His Word by living obedient lives is to ask Him to compromise His very nature. God cannot go against His own Word. He cannot reward disobedience or avert the consequences of our actions. God gave us His commandments — and there are more than ten — for our protection. They arose out of His love for us because He wanted to help us avoid loss, heartache, and bodily harm. God saw that certain reactions or consequences would accompany certain actions, and He deemed for the sake of those He cherished — us — that those actions should be avoided. He took the time to point out through Moses that if Israel did A, B would occur. But if they didn't do A, they would reap a less desirable result. Therefore, He said, *"Choose."* As I said before, you have a big say-so in how blessed you will be based upon the way you choose to live.

If you fully obey the LORD your God and carefully follow all his commands I give you today, the LORD your God will set you high above all the nations on earth. All these blessings will come upon you and accompany you if you obey the LORD your God. . . . However, if you do not obey the LORD your God and do not carefully follow all his commands and decrees I am giving you today, all these curses will come upon you and overtake you. (Deuteronomy 28:1–2,15)

So there it is. We either worship God in

spirit and walk out the truth of His commands, or we suffer the consequences of our sinful ways. I suggest you read Deuteronomy 28 for yourself, examine your options, and then joyfully choose life and blessings.

> Blessed are all who fear the LORD,
>   who walk in his ways.
> You will eat the fruit of your labor;
>   blessings and prosperity will be yours.
>   (Psalm 128:1–2)

> You come to the help of those who *gladly do right,*
>   who remember your ways.
>   (Isaiah 64:5)

Basically God is saying, "Hey, all I'm asking for is some respect and a heart that rejoices in being obedient to Me. Walk in reverence. Though I'm the friend who sticks closer than a brother, don't treat Me like a common buddy. I am God. Recognize the difference and conduct yourself accordingly. Don't be obedient to Me out of duty, being grudgingly religious and unpleasant. I would rather you joyfully fulfill my wishes because you love Me and sincerely want to make Me happy." That's not too much to ask, especially when we consider all He has done and all He has promised us.

THE BEST OF COMPANIONS

But perhaps this is where we miss it. We make costly mistakes because we lack knowledge. People don't deliberately choose to rob themselves of a blessing. This is why you must fill yourself with the knowledge of God's Word. Know what your heavenly Father likes and doesn't like, what your spiritual rights are. Satan takes advantage of what you don't know. He knows God's Word inside out, and he knows how to twist it in the hearts of those who are not soundly rooted in the knowledge of what God has to say about how to live.

How you live your life is based not only on *what* you know, but also on the influence of *whom* you know and with whom you choose to align yourself. Our companions can affect our ability to stay pure. Mary was pledged to be married to Joseph, a descendant of the house of David. He came from good stock. He was a member of the family of God. His lineage held a precious promise from the Lord. God had promised David that the throne would not depart from his family line. Joseph was the next man up. Therefore, in perfect accordance with what

God had pledged to David, Joseph was chosen to be the earthly father of the King of kings and Lord of lords. The people God places in our lives promote His kingdom design. But those we choose for ourselves can pull us off course by influencing us to listen to the voice of the flesh and the voices in the world that attempt to drown out the voice of the Holy Spirit.

The effect of being near sin is a lot like what happens when you're near people who smoke. Nonsmokers who spend any time in a smoke-filled room complain of smelling like an ashtray afterward. The smoke of others saturates their clothing, their hair, their skin. If you didn't know better, you would think they themselves had been smoking! I once lived in an apartment previously occupied by a smoker. Though the carpet had been cleaned many times, on sunny days when the temperature rose, the smell of smoke also rose and filled the room. Sin is that way. Though you yourself may not partake of the things your associates do, the smell of their deeds will cling to you. It will begin to penetrate your spirit and, ever so slowly, your attitude will become more and more like theirs. Solomon was a wise man until he surrounded himself with wives who worshiped idols. They eventually seduced him away from the God who had blessed him so extravagantly. We cannot avoid everybody in the world, but we can more carefully pick our circle of Christian friends.

> Don't you know that a little yeast works through the whole batch of dough? Get rid of the old yeast that you may be a new batch without yeast — as you really are. For Christ, our Passover lamb, has been sacrificed. Therefore let us keep the Festival, not with the old yeast, the yeast of malice and wickedness, but with bread without yeast, the bread of sincerity and truth.
>
> I have written you in my letter not to associate with sexually immoral people — not at all meaning the people of this world who are immoral, or the greedy and swindlers, or idolaters. In that case you would have to leave this world. But now I am writing you that you must not associate with anyone who calls himself a brother but is sexually immoral or greedy, an idolater or a slanderer, a drunkard or a swindler. With such a man *do not even eat.* (1 Corinthians 5:6–11)

Paul's words are seemingly harsh, but he knew that "evil companions corrupt

58

good manners." Or, as Proverbs 12:26 tells us, the way of the wicked leads the righteous man astray. Why did Paul say not to eat with such people? Because eating is a communion of sorts. It is the place where we relax. When we relax we become vulnerable, open to whatever is said or done. We cannot afford to relax in a world where the enemy of our souls is ever relentlessly on the prowl, like a lion, seeking whom he may devour. We must be ever alert.

Perhaps this is what Daniel and the Hebrew boys Shadrach, Meshach, and Abednego understood. Perhaps this is why they refused to eat the meats and sweets from the king's table. They chose to stick to the diet God had prescribed in His law. The difference between them and those who ate whatever they were served was clearly apparent — they were found to be in better health and far wiser than the others in the court. No doubt those who ate whatever they were served were quite sluggish from all their indulgent feasting. Daniel, along with Shadrach, Meshach, and Abednego, was blessed with a prominent position in the king's court that lasted through several different administrations. We never hear anymore about those who pigged out

— no pun intended.

WATCHING YOUR DIET

We cannot eat what the world eats and expect to be spiritually healthy. Indeed, what we feed the most will be the strongest. This is why the knowledge of God's Word is of the utmost importance. It is our only standard and foundation for godly living. Our spirit must be stronger than our flesh in order for us to live a pure and consecrated life before God. We must make sure that although we live in the world, we are not *of* the world. Jesus was so balanced in this. He understood that He had to eat physically, but His more crucial diet was a spiritual one. When assaulted by temptation He knew what God had said, and His Father's Word kept Him rooted in his faith.

> Jesus answered [Satan], "It is written: 'Man does not live on *bread alone,* but on every word that comes from the mouth of God.' " (Matthew 4:4)

Jesus walked among those in the world, ministered to them, and pointed them toward an eternal mind-set. Then He withdrew to spend His vulnerable time with His Father and those who were seeking God.

He built Himself up with His Father's words and made decisions based only upon His Father's advice. He did not listen to those who offered contrary suggestions. He ate the Word of God. He digested it and lived it. And He surrounded Himself with an inner circle of those who were striving to do the same.

I am convinced that godly companions also surrounded Mary. Her fiancé was a godly man who was able to hear and follow God. Her cousin Elizabeth was a godly woman who was able to believe God for her own miracle — a child in her old age, a very special child, John the Baptist, who would pave the way for Jesus Christ.

When you want to be successful, you should hang around successful people. Always take advice from those who have excelled at what you yourself are striving to do. If you want to live a holy life, then associate with those who are walking in the same direction. Be transparent and allow them to hold you accountable to the standard God sets before you.

Mary spent time with Elizabeth and received a confirmation that, yes, she was on the right path. That visitation from the angel was not a figment of her imagination — it was real. It was of God. Elizabeth had to have been a tremendous support to Mary as she faced this momentous event. Let's face it: She couldn't tell just anybody about her circumstances. Who would understand it?! *Pregnant by the Spirit of God? Come on, who are you trying to fool?* Her situation could have been made a mess if shared with the wrong person, namely, someone who wasn't walking in the Spirit. I'm sure Elizabeth counseled Mary on how to conduct herself until God had set all the pieces and players in place. Godly counsel is crucial to maintaining purity and faith in a world that constantly pulls at our flesh and our fears. If we're honest, it is our unbelief and fear that cause us to fall, to give in to moments of immediate gratification while ignoring the eternal ramifications.

Now, a lot of single women are probably struggling through this chapter. You are saying, "Michelle, I am not a virgin. Does that mean that God will not bless me? I've blown it. How can I salvage what has been lost?" I have good news for you. Through the blood of Jesus your virginity has been spiritually restored.

If anyone is in Christ, he is a *new* creation; the old has gone, the *new* has come! (2 Corinthians 5:17)

There is no need to wallow in mourning or to fall into self-condemnation. You are not alone in your struggles with the flesh. God is well aware that we are but dust. This is why He made a provision for our restoration.

Even David, the king of Israel who had an adulterous affair and committed murder to cover it up, was still called "a man after God's own heart." Certainly he was not perfect, but he was repentant. He confessed his sin (remember, confession goes beyond *admitting* what you did to saying what *God* says about what you did), accepted the consequences, submitted himself to the correction and chastening of the Lord, and did not repeat that offense again. Though he was a mighty warrior and king of a powerful nation, the only thing that truly mattered to him was the presence of God in his life. He could not stand the thought of facing another day without God. He did not consider himself too high to call out to the Lord.

> Cleanse me with hyssop, and I will be
>   clean;
>   wash me, and I will be whiter than
>   snow. . . .
> Hide your face from my sins

and blot out all my iniquity.
Create in me a pure heart, O God,
    and renew a steadfast spirit within me.
Do not cast me from your presence
    or take your Holy Spirit from me.
Restore to me the joy of your salvation
    and grant me a willing spirit, to sustain
    me. . . .
You do not delight in sacrifice, or I would
    bring it;
    you do not take pleasure in burnt
    offerings.
The sacrifices of God are a broken spirit;
    a broken and contrite heart,
    O God, you will not despise.
                        (Psalm 51:7,9–12,16–17)

David cried out to God, and the Lord heard him. Your repentance and your cry for forgiveness have been heard by God. God has thrown your sins as far as the east is from the west to be remembered no more. He has granted you a fresh start. A new beginning. A chance to get it right this time.

Don't get hung up on the terminology of virginity. Embrace the principle of purity from the inside out: A pure heart that leads to pure actions, actions that get the attention of God and please Him. Yes, Mary was a virgin physically, and some of us are not.

But Mary had something that we all can have — a clean heart and a right spirit. You see, the issue is not really physical virginity, it's spiritual chastity. Living a pure life. A godly life. The bottom line is that Mary did not offend God. This should be our daily goal. Remember, if you want to be blessed by someone, do not offend him or her.

THOUGHTS TO PONDER

- Are you walking in the awareness that you are promised to someone?

- How is your courtship with God going?

- If someone "smelled" you, would that person smell the smoke of the world or the fragrance of the Holy Spirit?

- Take inventory of those who form your inner circle of friends. Do they influence your spirit or your flesh? Which influence is strongest at this time?

- What spiritual food are you eating? What things in your diet need to change?

3. THE HEART OF THE FATHER

GRASPING WHAT GETS GOD'S ATTENTION

The angel went to [Mary] and said, "Greetings, you who are highly favored! The Lord is with you."

Luke 1:28

What a powerful phrase! "The Lord is with you!" Can you imagine how Mary felt?

E. V. Hill, one of the most respected preachers of our time, once preached a sermon in which he recounted an international trip he took with Jesse Jackson. Since Rev. Jackson was the celebrated guest on this excursion, all deference and protection was afforded to him. At times, as they went from place to place, the pastor and the statesman would be separated in the bustle of the crowd. As Pastor Hill tried to make his way back to the side of Rev. Jackson, security guards would circumvent his efforts until he said, "I'm with him." All the special treatment he received on the journey was because of his affiliation with the guest of honor. All entrées he enjoyed were because of his association with Rev. Jackson.

Pastor Hill concluded his sermon by saying that one day we would stand before the pearly gates of heaven. And as we head toward the open gate an angel will block our path. But because of Jesus we will be able to point toward the throne room where God resides and say, "I'm with Him." And on that declaration the angel will step aside and allow us into that great heavenly city. Well, I have to tell you I just shouted. It was such an incredible picture of what our association with the Lord really means.

LET US DRAW NEAR

The Lord was with Mary. And, oh, how we need His presence in our lives as well in order to be blessed! He is our entrée into the blessed and highly favored life. With Him as our escort we are blessed going in and blessed going out. Blessed when we sit and blessed when we rise. Which means we must invite Him into our midst. I've never seen a person willfully hang out uninvited with someone for very long. No one who understands their own worth would force himself or herself on an unwilling companion. Why go where you are tolerated when you can be celebrated somewhere else? God is a gentleman. He doesn't force Himself on anyone; He politely waits for an invitation to be a part of your life. He doesn't pry into your affairs. He waits for you to open the door.

> Come near to *God* and he will come near to you. (James 4:8)

> Here I am! I *stand* at the *door* and *knock.* If anyone hears my voice and opens the *door,* I will come in and eat with him, and he with me. (Revelation 3:20)

God has perfect etiquette. He will enter the parlor of your heart and abide there only by invitation. Obviously Mary had extended the invitation and the Lord had taken her up on it. Not only had she invited Him into her life, she celebrated His presence. Mary was a worshiper. She was being rewarded for diligently seeking the Lord. She worshiped God in spirit and in truth.

What does it mean to really worship God in spirit and in truth? Worshiping God goes beyond the worship service on Sunday morning. Worship is the rehearsing of God's Word continually. Meditating on it and living it twenty-four hours a day, seven days a week, three hundred sixty-five days a year. Worship is constant surrender to the Lord and living in agreement with His Word. That's right, talking the talk and walking the walk. Being living epistles for all to see. Our worship of God should affect our countenance, attitude, and actions. Worship is continually saying yes to God in every area of our lives.

Worship involves loving the unlovely, overlooking offenses, refusing to tell off someone who deserves it. Submitting to a difficult boss, to an even more difficult mate. Being kind to a hateful coworker. Blessing that driver who deliberately cut you off in traffic. Giving when you feel you don't really have it to give. Every occasion that you say yes to God and no to your natural inclinations, you are worshiping. Worship is maintaining an attitude of humility even when you have every right to feel proud. It is recognizing that all you have and all you are come from the hand of God. Now *that* is worship. Mary flowed in her worship. It bubbled up from her inner self like a fountain. It touched others. It was contagious to those around her. They were moved to praise God as well.

When Elizabeth heard Mary's greeting, the

baby leaped in her womb, and Elizabeth was filled with the Holy Spirit. In a loud voice she exclaimed: "Blessed are you among women, and blessed is the child you will bear! But why am I so favored, that the mother of my Lord should come to me? As soon as the sound of your greeting reached my ears, the baby in my womb leaped for joy." (Luke 1:41–44)

When you are a true worshiper, you affect people around you. They recognize the hand of God on your life. When you are a worshiper nothing is a coincidence, everything is a miracle, and you are quick to give the glory back to God. Mary knew the source of her blessings and loudly proclaimed it.

My soul glorifies the Lord,
   and my spirit rejoices in God my Savior,
for he has been mindful
   of the humble state of his servant.
From now on all generations will call me
    blessed,
   for the Mighty One has done great
   things for me —
   holy is his name.
His mercy extends to those who fear him,

from generation to generation.
(Luke 1:46–50)

There was no claiming credit or leaving the conclusion to chance in Mary's proclamation. She understood that those who fear the Lord receive His mercy and that those who worship God receive a measure of blessings and favor above what can be measured or anticipated.

WHEN THE PRAISES GO UP

What is it about worship and praise? When the praises go up, the blessings come down, as the popular saying goes. Let's think about this. Don't you love being around those who have good things to say about you? You like those people, don't you? Why? Because they like you! Well, God loves to visit with those who love Him. However, praise is just the beginning for Him.

Know therefore that the LORD your God is God; he is the faithful God, keeping his covenant of *love* to a thousand generations of *those* who *love* him and keep his commands. (Deuteronomy 7:9)

Then I said: "O LORD, God of heaven, the great and awesome God, who keeps his covenant of *love* with *those* who *love* him and obey his commands." (Nehemiah 1:5)

Notice that loving Him and obeying Him are never separate in the Lord's eyes. He visits those who couple their praise with a worshipful, obedient life. God showed up for those whose hands and hearts were clean, for those whose lips acknowledged Him with the praise that is due Him. He showed up for those who truly wanted to see and to know Him. When Moses went into the Tent of Meetings to worship, God would come down. His presence would cover and fill the tent to overflowing. Those standing far off could see the glory of God from where they were. It was an awesome sight. God showed up for Moses so that the people of Israel would know that He had Moses' back, and they were to do as Moses instructed them. When God has your back, there should be no question about it to others around you.

Remember when Moses came down from the mountain after receiving the commandments and after spending time in the presence of God? His face was shining so brilliantly that the people had to step back. They couldn't look at him; they needed sunglasses! He had to cover his face with a veil. Your encounters with God should also be evident on your countenance. The evidence should be clear that He shows up in your daily life and in the circumstances you encounter.

OH, THE GLORY!

When Solomon dedicated the temple he had built to the Lord, everyone had assembled to worship Him. The priests had gathered to do service unto the Lord, the ark of the covenant had been set in its right place in the Holy of Holies, and then an awesome thing happened. As Solomon invited God to come and reside in this place built for Him, the glory of the Lord came down and filled the temple. It was so intense, so glorious, that no one could remain in the temple. The priests could not perform their duties, so overtaken were they by the presence of God! That is what praise and worship does.

When Solomon finished praying, fire came down from heaven and consumed the burnt offering and the sacrifices, and the *glory* of the LORD *filled* the temple. The priests could not enter the temple of the LORD because the *glory* of the LORD *filled* it. (2 Chronicles 7:1–2)

God comes down and dwells in the midst of our praise, in the midst of our righteous living. It pleases Him to take up residence in a worshipful life. It is important to note that a few specific actions prompted God's powerful visitation and instruction. Let's take a look.

First, a temple had been prepared for God. Your body is the temple of the Holy Spirit. Have you prepared your temple to receive Him? Is it a place He would like to enter and abide?

Next, the ark of the covenant was put in its place. Is your covenant with God intact? Solomon prayed a prayer of dedication to the Lord, acknowledging His full ownership of the temple. Have you completely dedicated your life, your love, your all to Him? Do you love God with all your heart, all your soul, all your mind, and all your strength? Does your temple really belong to Him? Covenant is a serious matter to God, a matter of life and death. When God sealed His vow to Abraham, He walked between the separated halves of a dead animal, a gesture that meant, in essence, if I do not keep my promise let me be as this animal is — dead and cut off even from itself (Genesis 15:9–21).

Then sacrifices and burnt offerings were

rendered unto the Lord. Is your life all about you, or are you willing to sacrifice the desires of your flesh to obey the Word of the Lord? God prefers cheerful obedience over sacrifice. It delights His heart when He knows that we are happy to be obedient to Him, not out of religious duty but to honor our relationship with Him. Religious people are not happy people. They are unpleasant because they find no joy in what they do. They are motivated by the letter of the law, which kills. I encourage you to be motivated to obedience by love. The spirit of love will give life to your relationship with God and joy to your heart.

When all these things are in place, a miraculous thing occurs: God's glory fills your life. His presence so saturates you that it pushes some things out to make room for Him and for all that He wants to accomplish in your life. Remember those priests who couldn't go into the temple to perform their duties? The Spirit of God had overcome them, leaving no room for human effort, no room for manipulations to drum up the presence of God. No, God was taking over. He showed up and showed out — He performed extraordinarily! There was no disputing His awesome presence that day; it was clearly apparent to all in attendance.

Nothing else needed to be said or done. No pleas or requests needed to be voiced. Thoughts of lack or difficulty were banished when God visited. And that's what He still does! When He comes onto the scene, everything we want, need, or are looking and longing for comes with Him.

JESUS IN THE HOUSE

I was recently at a church where the congregants were encouraged to call out for money. There they were, calling money to themselves like calling a puppy. I was a bit bewildered by this. After all, if money could hear, that was news to me. We don't need to call forth inanimate objects. We simply need to seek God and make our requests known to him. When God comes on the scene, prosperity comes with Him. Healing comes. Joy comes. You name it. It comes as part and parcel of who He is. Not only does He have the whole world in His hands, He has everything we need in His hands.

You have made known to me the path of
   life;
   you will fill me with joy in your
   presence,

with eternal pleasures at your right
  hand.
                          (Psalm 16:11)

Surely you have granted him eternal
  blessings
and made him glad with the joy of your
  presence.
                           (Psalm 21:6)

If you say you want the blessings of God,
then what you really want is the presence of
God in your life. In His presence all perfect
gifts are found. I think of Esther, who had a
life-and-death problem on her hands. So
she fasted and prayed for three days. Then
she put on her royal robes and went into
the inner court to see her husband the king.
Well, when he saw her he was pleased with
her, extended his royal scepter to her, and
asked her what she wanted. He would give
her up to half of his kingdom if she wanted
it. Whew! Don't you want a dress like the
one she was wearing? It must have been
something else to get a reaction like that.
However, if I were to spiritualize this little
scenario, I would have to say that our King
is pleased to see us when we come into His
inner court wearing robes of righteousness,
an attitude of humility, a willingness to

77

serve, and a worshipful spirit.

Esther then served the king a fine banquet and made sure that his every need had been satisfied. In return, the king asked what he could do for her. Still she held back her request, simply inviting him to come to dinner again! After the second meal the king was feeling so good he again asked her what could he give her. She had brought so much pleasure to his senses that he wanted to reciprocate. When we have made the heart of God full with our worship, our service, and our submission to His Lordship, He, too, asks, "What can I do for you? It is My pleasure to give you the kingdom!"

Have you placed the things that please God above your own desires? Do you curry His favor? What set Joseph, the son of Jacob, apart from his brothers? What did he do to earn that coat of many colors? The coat represented far more than the favoritism of his father; it signified authority. Small wonder Joseph's brothers hated him. Yet Joseph sought the affection of his father by being the good son, so to speak. Joseph was the one his father relied on. Joseph honored his father. Jacob trusted Joseph with all that belonged to him. Why? Because Joseph drew close to Jacob's heart. He enjoyed being in the presence of his father. Jacob knew he had the undivided affections of his son. Can God say the same about you?

And what about King David? As I have mentioned before, he was no angel, yet God had a thing for David. He blessed David abundantly and secured an eternal legacy for his family. What was that all about? Well, think about it. Some call David the romantic warrior. He was always singing songs of worship to God. In his moments of extreme difficulty and fear, David chronicled his complaints, but he always ended by focusing on the abilities and mercies of God. David was a serious worshiper. And when he was wrong, he admitted it and was willing to accept the consequences.

After David angered God by taking a census, he realized the entire nation would suffer because of his decision. He asked God not to punish Israel for his sin. He made plans to buy a threshing floor so he could make a sacrifice to the Lord there and put an end to God's judgment. The owner of the floor offered to give it to David.

But the king replied to Araunah, "No, I insist on paying you for it. I will not *sacrifice* to the LORD my God burnt offerings that *cost* me nothing." So David bought the threshing floor and the oxen and paid fifty shekels of silver for them. (2 Samuel 24:24)

But King David replied to Araunah, "No, I insist on paying the full price. I will not take for the LORD what is yours, or *sacrifice* a burnt offering that costs me nothing." (1 Chronicles 21:24)

David refused to be cheap with God. True worshipers know that they owe everything they have to God, and they hold back no part of their possessions or themselves. Remember, this is the same man who danced right out of his clothes in public, so unadulterated was his worship of the King of all creation. He who was king became a commoner in the sight of his heavenly King. Though David was king of Israel, he still humbled himself before the Lord of the universe gladly and with complete abandon. He held nothing back. His heart was an open door, giving God free reign to come and go as He pleased, to give and take whatever He desired. David was transparent in his worship. God knew He could trust David with any blessing because He knew David would gladly give it back. Because David withheld nothing, God knew He could give him everything.

God could say the same about Mary. He knew He could trust her to be the mother of His Son because He knew her whole heart belonged to Him. She drew near to God and sought Him in every circumstance. She was in constant communion with Him, open to His every word and instruction. She was a yielded vessel awaiting His visitation. Everything about her countenance, the way she carried herself, her walk and her talk said, *Yes, Lord.* Mary delighted God because He knew He had her attention. Her thoughts were oriented toward Him continually. From all that the scriptures indicate to me, I feel it is safe to conclude that Mary had surrendered to God all rights to her life. Therefore He knew that He could use her.

You see, true worshipers are unselfish. They will not superimpose their personal agenda over God's kingdom purposes. Their focus is solely on pleasing their Beloved. The only thing they long for more of is God Himself. Why? Because they've tapped into a secret.

Thou wilt show me the path of life: In thy presence is *fullness* of *joy;* In thy right hand there are pleasures for evermore. (Psalm 16:11, ASV)

81

It doesn't get any better than that: fullness of joy, "pleasures evermore," as one translation says — I can go for all that, can't you?

Several friends I can think of bring me joy and pleasure. I want to be around them as much as possible because they brighten my day. When I'm not with them and I am in a situation I know they would enjoy, I think of them and make a mental note to repeat the activity with them. My thoughts are toward them because of the way I feel when I am with them. I reach out to them and do whatever I can to reciprocate the good times they have afforded me.

I believe that God is like that. When we bring Him joy and give Him pleasure, He thinks of all kinds of ways to reciprocate. When He knows that He is the center of our affection and that our hearts belong completely to Him, He knows that we will not be unfaithful lovers who squander His gifts. Then He freely gives without reservation. Yes, Mary could indeed magnify the Lord and sing of His faithfulness. He had answered her invitation to draw close to her. He had entered her personal space, searched her heart through and through, and found nothing wanting. They were intimate friends and confidantes. There were no secrets between Mary and her Lord. And so He chose to embrace her and deposit His Spirit within her to birth an extension of Himself — His only begotten Son. This was the most precious gift He could give her. The privilege of bearing what would be manifest to the world — His Word, living and breathing. Reflecting Him in the flesh. She would be the one who would feel His hand and His favor upon her. Not because of anything she did, but because of who she was.

A worshiper.

THOUGHTS TO PONDER

- Are you a worshiper? What does your worship entail?

- Is your goal to put a smile on God's face every day? Are you filled with thoughts of pleasing Him?

- Are God's plans and desires foremost in your heart? Where does your personal agenda fit in with His design? What place in your heart does His kingdom purpose occupy?

- What in life is most important to you? Do you feel that you have completely surrendered your desires and goals to God?

- What does your worship cost you? Is God's blessing worth the sacrifice?

4. EARS TO HEAR

DISCERNING THE WORD OF
THE LORD

Mary was greatly troubled at his words and wondered what kind of greeting this might be. But the angel said to her, "Do not be afraid, Mary, you have found favor with God."

Luke 1:29–30

Can you imagine? There sat Mary talking *— with an angel!* When was the last time *you* saw an angel? This has always blown my mind! It takes a special pair of eyes to be able to see past flesh and blood into the realm of the spirit. This experience is reserved for true worshipers who cross over the portal of their fleshly limitations in order to press into the presence of God. This is for the determined. Those who have made up their mind to see God. These worshipers don't intellectualize God. They are open to the moving of His Spirit yet are grounded in His Word. They press into His presence until they get a word from Him. So great is their longing to hear from heaven they forsake all other distractions and make the time to wait on Him. These are the ones God meets. And when He comes, He speaks profound truths that enable them to fulfill His kingdom purposes. He's no heavenly psychic who's going to tell you what your man did last night. Such so-called "spiritualists" summon and get their information from "familiar" or demonic spirits. To venture into that arena can be dangerous. Remember, God is not a gossip or a soothsayer. When He speaks, He has a totally different conversation for our spirits to hear. His thoughts are higher than our thoughts and always Kingdom focused — even when giving us a personal word.

True worshipers are spiritually sensitive because they constantly practice the presence of God. They don't talk *at* God, they talk *to* Him. Then they stop, wait, and listen for an answer. They understand that prayer time is a time for *conversation* with God, not a one-sided monologue. The intimacy that is birthed during this time of regular exchange primes their spirit and the ears of their inner being to hear and know His voice. And when they are not in conversation with God, they are still mulling over, meditating, and rehearsing His words.

True worshipers recognize God's voice and that of His messengers. Think about it. You can easily recognize the voices of those you know well. Even if they try to disguise it you would be quick to say, "Oh, so-and-so, I know that's you!" Your close friends don't have to announce who they are when they call you on the phone because you have spent so much time together that you recognize the tiniest inflection of their voices.

HEAR WHAT THE SPIRIT SAYS

What about people who commit terrible crimes and swear God told them to do it? Obviously they got their wires crossed! So how *does* one know when the Spirit of God is speaking to them? Simple. God never goes against His Word. He will never suggest or command something that doesn't line up with His written Word. Some might wonder about the instance when God told Abraham to sacrifice Isaac, but two important points apply to this case: First of all, God's Word was not yet documented. Second, God did not allow Abraham to complete the mission, thus being consistent with His Word even before it was written. He supplied a ram in the bush to be the sacrifice

He had requested. God's command was simply a test for Abraham. Would he be willing to give to God what was dearest to Him? The answer was yes.

Since then, the Word has been preserved for our benefit so that on days when the noise of the world drowns out the voice of God or robs us of our ability to discern the leading of His Holy Spirit, we have a written mandate that renders us without excuse. This is why it is so important to know the Scriptures through and through, not in part but the whole.

> *Study* to shew thyself *approved* unto God, a workman that needeth not to be ashamed, rightly dividing the word of truth. (2 Timothy 2:15, KJV)

> The *sum* of Thy word is truth,
> And every one of Thy righteous
>   ordinances is everlasting.
>   (Psalm 119:160, NASB)

Taking bits and pieces of God's Word out of the context of its entirety is dangerous. If you overhear a portion of a conversation, you are at risk of misunderstanding the overall content. This is why we must not dissect the Word of God without having a solid understanding of the whole. I always urge people to find a version of the Bible that is easy for them to comprehend, and then to read it all the way through like a novel before studying it topic by topic or book by book. This way you can see the big picture of God's heart and know that He is consistent in His views. Contrary to popular belief, the Bible does not contradict itself. God is not a schizophrenic God, one day feeling this way, the next day doing a total flip on us. No. He sticks to His guns. The disciple James said that God is so constant He doesn't change like shifting shadows (James 1:17). He is not moody. He remains true to Himself, to His Word. He is true to His Word because He *is* the Word. And that, my friend, is that!

But let's get back to recognizing God's voice. Knowing His mind and heart through His Word is crucial. What you know to be true about people makes a great difference in how you receive news or rumors about them. If someone delivered a message to you from your best friend and the content of that message was completely against his or her nature, the first thing you would say is, "That doesn't sound like my friend. I don't believe my friend said that! Let me double-check. You couldn't possibly have

89

gotten that right." You would not receive a bad rumor about your friend because you know your friend's usual behavior. You have walked and talked with that person enough to know what he or she is likely to do or not do. If someone asked you how your friend would feel about a certain matter, you would know or could at least make a close guess.

We must know God's character just as well as we know our friend's character. If someone said God told her something that goes against His Word, you shouldn't have to think about it. By instinct you should reply, "That doesn't sound like God to me. He wouldn't say that."

We grow acquainted with God when we spend time in prayer conversing with Him, and He with us. We know when He is on the scene. We learn how He communicates with us: through His Word, by His Spirit, through dreams and visions, or by the confirming words of others who walk in the Spirit and give sound counsel.

And it shall come to pass afterward, *that* I will pour out my spirit upon all flesh; and your sons and your daughters shall prophesy, your old men shall dream *dreams,*